I0062784

ANNE WALSH

HATE EXCEL?

WORK BOOK

Learn to love the software that can transform
your confidence and career

HATE

HOW TO USE THIS WORKBOOK

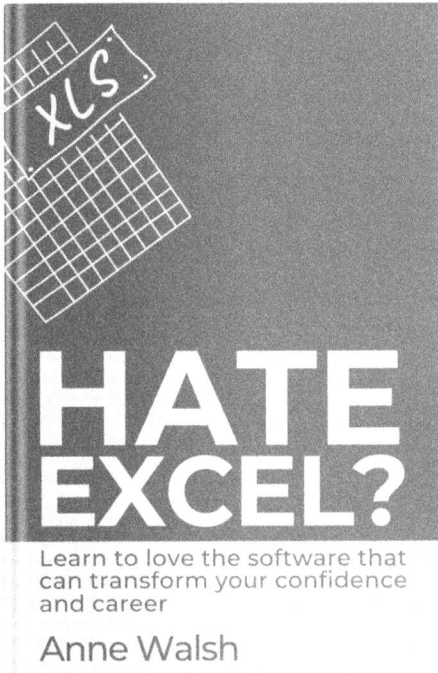

This workbook is made to accompany the book *"Hate Excel? Learn to love the software that can transform your confidence and career"*.

If you haven't got the book already, head over now to www.HateExcel.com. You will need to either have the receiptnumber from Amazon or use 16534 (that's the number of columns in an Excel spreadsheet – but you knew that didn't you?)

WWW.HATEEXCEL.COM

EXCEL

MORE ABOUT...

About *Hate Excel? Learn to love the software that can transform your confidence and career.*

This is a book about Excel and is for the person who has had Excel (like greatness), thrust upon them. The book tells you about Spreadsheet Sheila who, like a great detective learns to solve the Case of The Work Spreadsheet. Unlike most Excel books, it doesn't have loads of formulas, functions and How Tos..

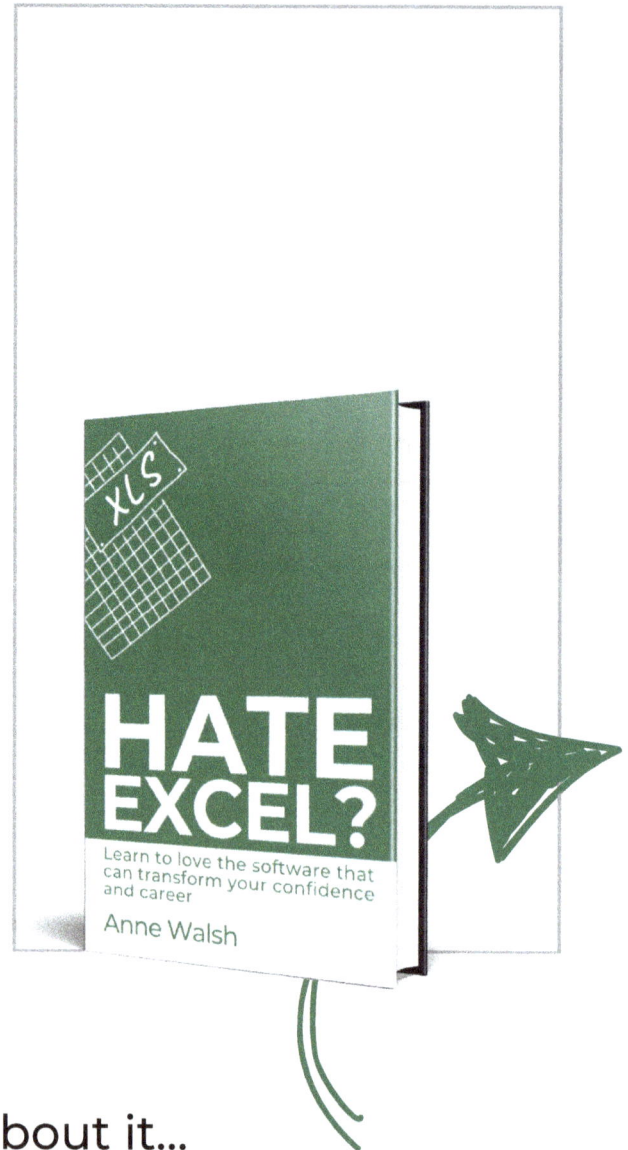

Here is what other people say about it...

XLS

HATE EXCEL?

Learn to love the software that can transform your confidence and career

Anne Walsh

★ CUSTOMERS SAY

👤 Emma Williams

★★★★★ **Excel-lent from an author who loves cells and puns**

Reviewed in the United Kingdom on October 17, 2024

Verified Purchase

If you hate Excel you are in the right place and plenty of good company. Most of us have to use it. But most of us haven't been taught it. What doesn't help is nerd-splaining from Alex in IT. That just raises the fears and the impostor syndrome.

👤 Matt

★★★★★ **Awesome book! Excellent read - very informative**

Reviewed in Australia on October 17, 2024

Verified Purchase

"Hate Excel" by Anne Walsh is a brilliantly relatable take on the daily struggles with Excel. Anne's witty style and practical tips make even the most frustrating tasks easier to handle. Her blend of humour and helpful advice makes this book a must-read for anyone who deals with Excel regularly.

Walsh turns the challenges of spreadsheet life into something you can laugh at, all while offering real solutions. A fun, insightful guide that's both entertaining and practical! Highly recommended for anyone looking to improve their Excel skills and have a good laugh along the way.

👤 Jennifer Louden

★★★★★ **Anne made me understand Excel - it's a miracle**

Reviewed in the United States on October 17, 2024

With empathy, humor, and love, Anne Walsh made me, ME! of all people, stop cowering in fear and feeling stupid when I have to even open an Excel spreadsheet. She helped me understand Excel which really does feel like a miracle. For those of us who aren't numbers-oriented, Excel can bring up so many bad memories of failing at math class and feeling so ashamed. Anne understands that.

WHO I AM

I always said that Excel picked me. I have been teaching Excel since the mid-1990s (from Excel 5.0) and have been a Master Instructor and a Microsoft Certified Trainer. Most importantly of all, I have done more than 10,000 hours as a trainer. I have written 8 books on Excel.

What I have seen over and over again is how much suffering people experience with Excel. It is not taught and yet somehow people are expected to know it. People hold themselves back, will not try for a job or promotion that they are well qualified for because "Good Excel Skills are required".

I see people spending 3 days every month on something that should take a maximum of a couple of hours because they do not have the Excel skills to do it. Time that could be better spent on something else.

As a trainer, I like to "put the fun in functions" and help learners feel free to experiment with Excel. I want it to be, as they say in Ireland, "a bit of craic".

You can read some testimonials for my work here.

If you would like to have a chat with me about delivering some Excel or PowerBI training for your organization – use this form to drop me a line

"*I am always doing that which I cannot do, in order that I may learn how to do it.*"

—Pablo Picasso

"Start by doing what's necessary; then do what's possible; and suddenly you are doing the impossible."

—St. Francis of Assisi

01 SHAME, THE BIG DRIVER

Identify your TWS
(The Work Spreadsheet) - Specifications

You may have more than one "Work spreadsheet" but there will probably be one that is the top priority. Choose that one.

What figures (exactly) do you need to get from the spreadsheet.

How often do they need to be produced e.g. monthly/weekly/ad hoc

What's the cut off time for them e.g. up to month end? Friday at 5pm?

Do they need to be presented in a specific template? Where can you get that template?

Make a note of the location here.

TWS – (The Work Spreadsheet)

Can you get access to a previous version?

Can the previous incumbent help you with it or would he/she/they be willing to record themselves doing it? Put their details e.g. email and phone number here.

If they don't have time to do that, can they tell you what formulas and functions they used?

Click on the cells with formulas and take a note of what the formula is:

Open your Work Spreadsheet. Click on the cell with the formula. Check the formula bar (top of screen). Highlight the formula (excluding the = at the beginning). Press Ctrl and C to copy. Then navigate to here and press Ctrl and V to paste it in.

Download the checklist. You will find this under the Chapter One Resources. Look for The Work Spreadsheet checklist.

Some extra help

Who have you chosen as your mentor? Real or imagined. Someone who will help you keep going when you really don't want to. Why have you chosen him/her/them?

Is there anyone in your organisation/network who could help you?
Write down some candidates here.

Can you identify any useful online resources? Ask the Excel people in your organisation who they would recommend online.

Go to your AI tool of choice, copy and paste in the formula and ask it to explain to you exactly what the formula does.

Capture your learnings

What are the key things you have learned? This is just for you.

Head over to www.the-excel-lady.com where I have lots of free excel tutorials.

"I am my own experiment.
I am my own work of art."

—Madonna

02 VISITING THE CRIME SCENE

Revisit your Work spreadsheet

Revisit the questions from the first chapter.
You could use The Work Spreadsheet checklist to help you.

Are you clearer now on what needs to be done with this spreadsheet?
Capture your thoughts here.

Perform some short - like a donkey's gallop – experiments

Open up Excel and rest your mouse on some of the icons at the top of the screen. Note that they tell you what they do. Don't worry if you don't know what a lot of them mean. This is acclimatisation. Write down here any of them that caught your fancy or that you recognised.

Go to **File** | **New** and have a look at the pre-set templates there. See if there are any that interest you. One of my favourites is the house cleaning check list. #JustSaying. Which ones did you download or have a look at?

Keep on working through the Quick Start course – this will be particularly helpful if you are new to Excel. It is designed to be less than an hour so you could do it at lunchtime. Any thoughts/observations/successes?

You will find access to the Excel Quick Start course under the **Chapter One Resources**. Remember it is free if you use the code **HateExcelBook**.

Head over to www.hateexcel.com to get access to your resources. You *have* bought the book haven't you?

Workplace courses – have you spoken to anyone about any workplace courses that are available/funded by your workplace. When can you sign up for them? Ideally check if they are recorded.

If someone in your company would like to speak to me about bringing me in as a trainer, you can email me at anne@the-excel-lady.com

Have you checked out my book?

Your Excel Survival Kit: Your guide to surviving and thriving in an Excel world.

It's available on Amazon. It got good reviews and they are not all from my mother...

Check it out here: https://amzn.to/3TVukeG

Capture your learnings

What are the key things you have learned? This is just for you.

"The true method of knowledge is experiment."

—William Blake

"There is no such thing as a failed experiment, only experiments with unexpected outcomes."

—Richard Buckminster Fuller

03 IT'S A PUZZLE, NOT A PUNISHMENT

Can you replicate any of the formulas in your Work Spreadsheet?
Remember to save a copy of the file and work on the copy.

You can find out how to save a copy in Module 3.4 of Excel Quick Start course.
You can also find a video on it under Chapter Two of the Hate Excel Book resources.

Remember – "Surgeons start with cadavers, not real people." How did it go?

What worked? How good did that feel? One of life's great pleasures – getting Excel formulas to work.

What didn't work? Were you able to figure out why? Maybe there is someone in your office who could help? The tutor on the course you are doing? Chat GPT/AI tool of choice?

What patterns if any are you noticing?

Have any of the common errors appeared?
Again, you can view those under the **Chapter Three resources.**

How are you feeling about the **Usual Suspects**? They are the list of topics that tend to come up over and over again. Again, you can view those under the **Chapter Three resources**.

My Big Board list

Compile **your** list of favourite books/resources here

If you don't have one, here is a list of ones I can recommend.

https://the-excel-lady.com/recommended-resources/

Capture your learnings

What are the key things you have learned? This is just for you.

Head over to www.the-excel-lady.com
where I have lots of free excel tutorials.

"Our key to transforming anything lies in our ability to reframe it."

— Marianne Williamson

04 REVISIT THE SCENE

Recognising your own thinking

At this stage, you probably know the thoughts and feelings that come up when you have to deal with an Excel spreadsheet. You can write them down here. Or if you prefer, do it on another page which you could dispose of safely.

> *"Until you're ready to look foolish, you'll never have the possibility of being great."* —Cher

Check under your Chapter Four resources to do the quiz on your favourite Excel story or you could click here.

Can I get me a reframe?

Part of the challenge you will face is that this is hard and confusing at times. A big part of your success is what you tell yourself about this challenge. Are you going to tell yourself one of the Ten Stories and so hate Excel for the rest of your life or are you going to tell yourself –

- I can do this.
- I can learn hard things.
- I can be a good example for my family with this.
- I won't let this beat me.

Only YOU know what would be a meaningful reframe for you. As I said in the story at the start of this book, shame was a big driver for me and still is quite often.

> *"A reframe is not about telling yourself that your fear is wrong. Reframes are about finding another way to look at the possibilities of your life."*
>
> —Rebecca K. Sampson,
> Self-Help Author

What can be the empowering thing you can tell yourself about learning Excel?

What can help remind you of your new story?
It could be a quote/an image – only YOU know what works for you.

What can I do in different timeslots?

> *"A small daily task, if it be really daily, will beat the labours of a spasmodic Hercules"* — Anthony Trollope – An Autobiography

Set yourself up for success. Identify what you can do in a number of different time slots. Here are some ideas.

Timeslot	5 things I can do	Comments/Observations
5 minutes	1. Review the Ribbon and note the names of the different icons 2. Experiment with typing in some text and formatting it 3. Make sure I know how to save/open/save a file under a different name 4. Search the File | New for an interesting download 5. Open the Quick Start course and have a look	
10 minutes	1. Experiment with typing in some numbers and formatting them 2. Learn 3 Excel keyboard shortcuts 3. Skim read the chapter of an Excel book 4. Complete a topic from the QuickStart course 5. Watch a video on YouTube	

Timeslot	5 things I can do	Comments/Observations
15 minutes	1. Check the help on a topic 2. Work through a tutorial on a previously unknown topic 3. Review notes on the work spreadsheet and identify topic I need to brush up on 4. Learn about "fixing" a cell 5. Learn 5 Excel keyboard shortcuts	
20 minutes	1. Google a topic from "The Usual Suspects" 2. Try out the Excel snacks from Chapter Five resources 3. Ask Chat GPT or AI tool of your choice to explain a formula to you 4. Work through a chapter of a book 5. Ask someone in your office to explain their spreadsheet to you	
30 minutes	1. Start working through the practice files for Chapter Six 2. Experiment with recording yourself doing something on Teams/Zoom (Chapter Seven resources) 3. Come up with the first draft of your own learning plan 4. Work through some of the vlookup materials from the Chapter One resources 5. Experiment with some of the options in the formula cheatsheet (Chapter two)	

Now devise your own list.

Timeslot	5 things I can do	Comments/Observations
5 minutes		
10 minutes		
15 minutes		
20 minutes		
25 minutes		
30 minutes		

Capture your learnings

What are the key things you have learned? This is just for you.

"*Always plan ahead. It wasn't raining when Noah built the ark.*"

—Richard Cushing

05 CLOSING IN ON THE SUSPECTS

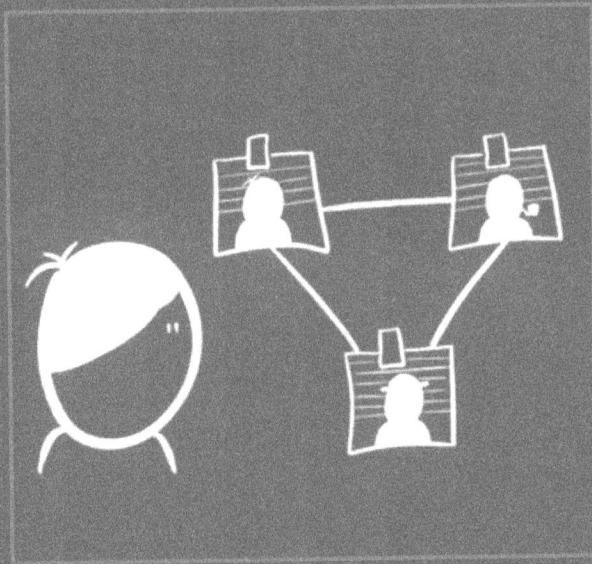

Four Tendencies Quiz

https://gretchenrubin.com/quiz/the-four-tendencies-quiz/

OK, so what type are you? I'm an Upholder which means I get s*** done but also means that I tend to keep going on the wrong path for much longer than I should because I have committed to it.

Write down your thoughts here about your type.

What's YOUR Why?

There is a story about Marlon Brando in the later days of his career, who when he was asked about his motivation pointed to a big pile of money…and said "That's my motivation"

This exercise suggest that you use Chat-GPT (or the AI tool of your choice) to explore your own deeper motivation. Again, this is JUST for you.

You will find it under your Chapter Five Resources (ChatGPT prompt to help you identify your why)

But When?

Use this as a template at the start of each week. Things are more likely to happen if you schedule them into your diary. If you are doing a class, consider building in "after time" to review what you have learned. Remember the Ebbinghaus forgetting curve. You can google that one.

Learn more about your Tendency (Upholder, Rebel, Obliger and Questioner) and what can help you to stay on track.

This link can give you some ideas: https://gretchenrubin.com/four-tendencies/

"Someone's sitting in the shade today because someone planted a tree a long time ago."

—Warren Buffett

Day	Topic	What I want to do	How much time I have

How?

> *"We discover through working what we cannot discover any other way."*
> **—James Baldwin**

In my opinion, the only real way to learn Excel is to actually do exercises and practise it. As I observe many times in class.

"I can watch gymnastics all day long. It won't make me a gymnast" – Anne Walsh
Again, get superclear about what you are going to do e.g do my homework. Try the exercise from a video.

Another piece that is very important to know. YOU WILL FAIL. Formulas won't work, Excel will do weird stuff.

Have your list of go-to strategies.

- Check your Why.
- Be willing to stop and start again.
- Deep breath and positive self-talk.

Write down your list of 3-4 go to strategies to help when things go wrong.

Where?

This is worth considering. Here are some questions to ponder.

- Home or work?
- Do you have a home office you could use?
- Do you have access to a computer with Excel on it?
  - No, Google sheets is not the same. Let me give you an analogy. If you are learning to drive, do you want to learn on the same car every week or a different one? When you can drive, it doesn't make much difference. Until you can, it really does affect you.
- Can you do it in your office or can you move to a quieter location?
- Are there quiet times in your office/home that you can avail of?
- Do you want to work by yourself or with others?

What are my optimal locations for my learning?

Who? – Who can be my E-Team?

These will be the people who can help you if you get stuck. Here are some ideas from the book.

- Someone from the IT department (please bear in mind that they may or may not have Excel expertise and their primary role is NOT to help you with Excel)
- Resident Excel God/dess
- Your instructor if you are attending a course.
- A role model from the Internet
- Excel forums

Something worth considering here is that different people may (like your friendships) be more helpful in different roles.

Here is my E-Team

Name	Email/Phone/website	How they can help me best and when

Have you thought about your Training Temptations?

It is wise to consider what might derail you. Again, this is different for different people. Have a go at the Training Temptations quiz here. This should offer you some insight.

You will find the link under the Chapter Five resources or you can click here.
https://the-excel-lady.com/excel-training-temptations-quiz/

As we all know, an ounce of prevention is worth a pound of cure. Although "cure" can be way sexier than "prevention".

Part of this work is learning to recognise your own temptations and put strategies in place to make it easier for yourself. If you are going on a healthy eating kick, it's much easier to do if you get rid of the junk food and have healthy food already prepared.

Have a look at this sample **When Then** table.

When	Then
I need 15 minutes to review my work and I know the phone will be ringing	Ask a colleague to help (and be sure to return the favour) and/or set up a voice mail
I am hangry (cranky and hungry)	I get something to eat, go for a quick walk and then choose a 5 minute exercise to do
I feel tempted to solve other people's problems instead of doing my homework	Remind myself that I need to "put on my own mask first"
I want to get someone to do it for me rather than doing it myself	I have a go and then I ask the God/dess if I get stuck
I can feel an old story starting up	Have a list of reframes and positive self-talk ready

What are your **When Then** options.

When	Then

Rewarding your successes/efforts

I have to admit, I am not very good at this. This is as much for you as it is for me. This is something very personal. These are some ideas of what would constitute rewards for me. YOU might have a completely different list.

- A cup of really strong tea
- A mincemeat pie – yes, I know they are a Christmas thing but they taste great all year round.
- Episode of something from Netflix
- A print of something I really love.
- New drawing pencils.
- Celebrity magazine.
- New detective novel.

What would be your rewards?

Capture your learnings

What are the key things you have learned? This is just for you.

"*Before anything else, preparation is the key to success.*"

—Alexander Graham Bell

06 WORKING THROUGH THE PLAN

"There are no failures – just experiences and your reactions to them."

—Tom Krause

At this point you have done lots of work on your mindset, come up with a plan, identified and neutralised your Training Temptations.

Now it's time for execution...not THAT sort of execution, although it may feel like that. As part of the resources of the book I have included files for you to work on. Now you are going to work on them. You can download them from Chapter Six Resources.

I suggest you draw up a plan for a week to start. Have a contingency plan because you know, well, life.

Here's a template to help you get started. See the next page.

Another thing to include is how you are going to reward yourself as you complete each bit. Put the focus on "doing the thing", which you *do* have control over, rather than the outcome – which you have *no* control over.

Date	What?	When?	How?

Where?	Who?	Possible obstacles	Workarounds

Review of the week

"Effective execution of a bad idea is better than the bad execution of a good idea." –Bill Gates

What worked?

What didn't work?

What will I do differently?

What do I need to keep reminding myself of?

How will I reward myself?

What "ahas"/lightbulb moments did I have – if any?

What did you learn about yourself? Any surprises?

Capture your learnings

What are the key things you have learned? This is just for you.

"*What we perceive as limitations have the potential to become strengths greater than what we had when we were 'normal' or unbroken. When something breaks, something greater often emerges from the cracks.*"

—Nnedi Okorafor – Broken Places
and Outer Spaces

07 ALL IS WELL THAT ENDS WELL AND ONTO THE NEXT CASE

Please pause here to acknowledge yourself. Learning Excel and having the courage to face your own fears around this is no small thing.

What I'd like to invite you to do now is to dream...you have taken on this big challenge. I strongly suspect that you are doing more with Excel than the person who began this workbook ever thought he/she could do...

What other goals could you accomplish that have felt beyond you?
What learnings could you take from this journey to apply to achieving that goal?

So what's possible now?
Dare to dream.....

"We all have possibilities we don't know about. We can do things we don't even dream we can do."

—Dale Carnegie

If you would like to connect..

www.the-excel-lady.com

Want to discuss training for your organisation?

🌐 https://the-excel-lady.com/contact/

in LinkedIn: https://www.linkedin.com/in/theexcellady/

✉ Contact me directly: anne@the-excel-lady.com

Copyright

© Anne Walsh Copyright 2025

All rights reserved. No part of this publication may be reproduced, stored in or introduced into a retrieval system, or transmitted, in any form, or by any means (electronic, mechanical, photocopying, recording or otherwise) without the prior written permission of the creator.

This book is sold subject to the condition that it shall not, by way of trade or otherwise, be lent, resold, hired out, or otherwise circulated without the publisher's prior consent in any form of binding or cover other than that in which it is published and without a similar condition including this condition being imposed on the subsequent Purchaser.

www.ingramcontent.com/pod-product-compliance
Lightning Source LLC
Chambersburg PA
CBHW051800200326
41597CB00025B/4630

* 9 7 8 1 9 0 8 7 7 0 8 0 6 *